THE BOOK OF HEAVENLY DEATH BY WALT WHITMAN COMPILED FROM LEAVES OF GRASS BY HORACE TRAUBEL

PORTLAND MAINE
THOMAS B MOSHER
MDCCCCV

The printed source of the material
used in this volume is the Small,
Maynard and Company edition of
Leaves of Grass, to which all the
page references that follow apply

H. T.

CONTENTS

CONTENTS

CONTENTS

xi

CONTENTS

xii

CONTENTS

The idea of this collection was first discussed by me with the late Herbert Small, of Small, Maynard and Company, Boston. I discovered later on that Thomas B. Mosher had independently conceived the same idea. I ought also to acknowledge in this place the editorial advisorship of Anne Montgomerie, Thomas B. Harned and Thomas B. Mosher.

H. T.

PREFACE

 HITMAN pronounced the last yes about death. He pushed aside the curtaining doctrines and sciences and said: Look. With him immortality was not an argument. It was a vision. Life does not answer the questions of reason. It answers the questions of sight. There was no because or therefore in Whitman's revelation. Everything about Whitman was this: See. See life. See love. See the soul. See the continuance of identity. See the past. See the future. See the sympathies. See. See. That was the Whitman attitude. What Spinoza said concerning God, "to reason about God is to deny him," Whitman said about immortality, to reason about immortality is to deny it. I have heard him say to a skeptic: "If I tried to prove things to myself I, too, would deny things. I do not prove things — I see things. Seeing is enough." He said to Ingersoll once in my presence: "Robert, logic is well enough, figures are well enough, but when I look at you, at myself, at anybody, I seem to see something better." The best things, the final things, the essential things, cannot, anyhow, be proved by a process but by vision. Whitman refused to be reasonable because of reason, as Schiller refused to be religious because of religion. He was not to be trapped into arguments and ballotings. He knew that after the heat of discussion, after the vote was in and counted, everything still remained unproved. What could authentically report on death? He claimed that death could be realized as life again only when the farthest removed from controversy. This is what he said to a disputant: "You prove that death is empty and then I see that it is full of life." "Death, mother," he said to an old woman we both knew, "death, you see, is not something that stops us but something that helps us on." A man of science asked him: "Do you think, Mr. Whitman, that immortality will ever be proved?" "Proved — in reality proved: yes. Proved as you understand proved: no. There are certain sorts of truths that may yield their own sort of evidences. Immortality is not speculative — it does not come in response to investigation —

PREFACE

it does not give its secret up to the chemist: immortality is revelation : it flashes itself upon your consciousness out of God knows what." If you asked Whitman whether he had reasons for his belief he would reply : " No reasons whatever — reasons would spoil it all." Whitman always quoted death like a man who stood way up somewhere and dared to speak of things that he saw. I remember that on one occasion he reflected fervently out loud in my hearing : " The best of what I have seen about death came once, long ago, all of a sudden." I never knew him at any time to consent to submit the question to any formal court or jury, scientific or metaphysical. He felt distinctly averse to the cross-examination involved — to the pros and cons, "the destructive confusions " as he called them, that resulted from the eagerness of counsellors to win their case. "You might just as well take love before a magistrate and have it committed for trial." He was perfectly willing to confess that his best faith would be convicted and sentenced in any court of formal logic. Yet the best faith would remain the best faith forever. " I know that I would go down under the first fire of attack. Any smart lawyer could make me contradict myself." He was rather impatient with an inquirer who declared that he " always insisted upon proofs " for his beliefs, whatever they were. Whitman replied : " So do I.

But what are proofs?" Finally he asserted with great vehemence: "I see! I see! I see! Seeing is enough!"

Whitman sometimes complained to me that many of his own friends had mistaken his philosophy about death. He did not speculate with the idea of an indefinite race immortality. He asserted a definite individual immortality. He wished to be understood as standing explicitly for this conclusion. Ingersoll said to him: "Whitman, I cannot argue out immortality." To this Whitman replied: "Neither can I." Ingersoll added: "I cannot see it." Whitman added: "I can *see* it." Ingersoll instantly caught the distinction. "I understand," he said. And then they were both silent. Commenting on Ingersoll's own view of immortality Whitman said: "Robert takes hold of the knob of the door, even turns the knob, but refuses to open the door." He said to a group of us together at a table when death was discussed: "It is all right for you fellows to distrust my eyesight if you choose, but I want you to acknowledge the honesty of my report." He insisted upon being quoted right. "Nowhere I look, this side of what we call death or the other, do I see the extinguishment, effacement, of the individual." He said to a young mother who cried about a lost boy: "Never mind Mary — the youngster will last till you get there and when you get there the two of you will last along together." I asked him if he thought his text was always as clear on that point as it might be. " Perhaps not. I have asked myself the same question. I have always wished to make it plain enough without making it too plain — plain enough to be understood but not sharp enough to become a dogma." He laughed over the matter in this way: " I have no thirty-nine articles about death to repeat: I have only one article: but I would prefer to have that one article clear as to the main point — beyond the range of clerical dispute." He was willing to be thought wrong but he was not willing to be considered in doubt. I was one evening saying good-night to him before going off to give a talk on Leaves of Grass in a church. He counselled me: " Whatever you say or do not say, be very sharp and positive in your affirmation of immortality. We must show the church itself that in the best item of its creed we can go it one better."

To Whitman a doubt of death was a doubt of life. He could not see life rounded without death to assist it. Nor could he see death rounded without life to assist it. He could not have seen reasons for the race if he had not seen reasons for the individual. He would not admit that either one needed to be obliterated for the sake of the other. The individual was continued. Whitman did not think what we call life mattered

PREFACE

or what we call death mattered. The individual survived both and was as God. His text provides for no peradventures. He tells us that if life is not life, then we have been fooled. Ring the bells, he says: wake up the people: tell them God has cheated them: tell them that nothing is worth while since God has not thought life was worth while. This was his if mood. But his affirmative nature never parlied with buts and maybes. He asserted the farthest providence of personal life. He did not look upon death as disintegrating the individual. Death simply passed the individual on. I used to say to him: "Have you any doubts at all about this?" And he would invariably answer: "None at all." Once he added: "If I doubted this I would doubt everything: I would have to recast my body and soul in the likeness of failure instead of the likeness of success."

Whitman did not invest in any sort of paradisaical preferments. Neither heaven nor hell came within the span of his vision. He saw eternal life — life persistently omnipotent. Life could not grant itself favors or exact penalties from itself. There was no afterworld of ecstasy or horror. There was an afterworld of men and women. Whitman was not incontinently harping upon good and bad, superior and inferior, god and devil, something to be worshipped and something to be hated. His future had no room for either the saved or the damned. It had room only for men and women. I sometimes went on in this style in his presence and he always seemed delighted. " That is the way to say it," he broke in upon my dispute with a third person — " that is the way to say it: death allows for no accidents, no withdrawals: death offers no options: the same gate is open to all — the same beyond is open to all." If there was anything he cared less for than the conventional brimstone it was the conventional altar fire. He often criticised religions but he never criticised religion. " I am the best friend of orthodoxy itself if orthodoxy only knew it — would listen long enough to really hear what I am saying. What do I say about death? Let me be vain and say: I say better things about death than orthodoxy with all its boasts is saying." Death neither stops nor starts anything. That was one of the declarations he was always making to me about death. Death was part of a process. Many deaths he sang. Many lives he sang. It seemed as though there was something greater than death, something greater than life, of which life and death were equal integers. Of that he finally sang. What was that something? Whitman does not answer with a table of figures. He answers with the soul.

HORACE TRAUBEL.

For life and death, for the Body and for the eternal Soul
Lo, I too am come.
Then falter not O Book, fulfil your destiny.

LEAVES OF GRASS.

THE BOOK OF HEAVENLY DEATH

I

THE SOUL,
    Forever and forever—longer than soil is brown
        and solid — longer than water ebbs and flows.

I will make the poems of materials, for I think
        they are to be the most spiritual poems,
And I will make the poems of my body and of mortality,
For I think I shall then supply myself with the poems of my
        soul and of immortality.

II

Each is not for its own sake,
I say the whole earth and all the stars in the sky are for
        religion's sake.

3

THE BOOK OF HEAVENLY DEATH

I say no man has ever yet been half devout enough,
None has ever yet adored or worship'd half enough,
None has begun to think how divine he himself is, and how
  certain the future is.

III

And I will show that there is no imperfection in the present,
  and can be none in the future,
And I will show that whatever happens to anybody it may
  be turn'd to beautiful results,
And I will show that nothing can happen more beautiful than
  death,
And I will thread a thread through my poems that time and
  events are compact,
And that all the things of the universe are perfect miracles,
  each as profound as any.

I will not make poems with reference to parts,
But I will make poems, songs, thoughts, with reference to
  ensemble,
And I will not sing with reference to a day, but with reference
  to all days,
And I will not make a poem nor the least part of a poem
  but has reference to the soul,

THE BOOK OF HEAVENLY DEATH

Because having look'd at the objects of the universe, I find
    there is no one nor any particle of one but has reference
    to the soul.

IV

I believe in you my soul, the other I am must not abase
    itself to you,
And you must not be abased to the other

Loafe with me on the grass, loose the stop from your throat,
Not words, not music or rhyme I want, not custom or lecture,
    not even the best,
Only the lull I like, the hum of your valvèd voice.

I mind how once we lay such a transparent summer morning,
How you settled your head athwart my hips and gently turn'd
    over upon me,
And parted the shirt from my bosom-bone, and plunged your
    tongue to my bare-stript heart,
And reach'd till you felt my beard, and reach'd till you held my
    feet.

Swiftly arose and spread around me the peace and knowledge
    that pass all the argument of the earth,
And I know that the hand of God is the promise of my own,
And I know that the spirit of God is the brother of my own,

And that all the men ever born are also my brothers, and the
    women my sisters and lovers,
And that a kelson of the creation is love.

V

Tenderly will I use you curling grass,
It may be you transpire from the breasts of young men,
It may be if I had known them I would have loved them,
It may be you are from old people, or from offspring taken soon
    out of their mothers' laps,
And here you are the mothers' laps.

VI

I wish I could translate the hints about the dead young men
    and women,
And the hints about old men and mothers, and the offspring
    taken soon out of their laps.

What do you think has become of the young and old men?
And what do you think has become of the women and children?

They are alive and well somewhere,
The smallest sprout shows there is really no death,
And if ever there was it led forward life, and does not wait at
    the end to arrest it,
And ceas'd the moment life appear'd.

THE BOOK OF HEAVENLY DEATH

All goes onward and outward, nothing collapses,
And to die is different from what any one supposed, and luckier.

Has any one supposed it lucky to be born?
I hasten to inform him or her it is just as lucky to die, and I
    know it.

I pass death with the dying and birth with the new-wash'd babe,
    and am not contain'd between my hat and boots,
And peruse manifold objects, no two alike and every one good,
The earth good and the stars good, and their adjuncts all good.

VII

I know I am deathless,
I know this orbit of mine cannot be swept by a carpenter's
    compass,
I know I shall not pass like a child's carlacue cut with a burnt
    stick at night.

VIII

And whether I come to my own to-day or in ten thousand or ten
    million years,
I can cheerfully take it now, or with equal cheerfulness I can wait.

My foothold is tenon'd and mortis'd in granite,
I laugh at what you call dissolution,
And I know the amplitude of time.

THE BOOK OF HEAVENLY DEATH

I am the poet of the Body and I am the poet of the Soul,
The pleasures of heaven are with me and the pains of hell are
  with me,
The first I graft and increase upon myself, the latter I translate
  into a new tongue.

IX

To any one dying, thither I speed and twist the knob of the door,
Turn the bed-clothes toward the foot of the bed,
Let the physician and the priest go home.

I seize the descending man and raise him with resistless will,
O despairer, here is my neck,
By God, you shall not go down ! hang your whole weight upon me.

I dilate you with tremendous breath, I buoy you up,
Every room of the house do I fill with an arm'd force,
Lovers of me, bafflers of graves.

X

Each who passes is consider'd, each who stops is consider'd,
  not a single one can fail.

It cannot fail the young man who died and was buried,
Nor the young woman who died and was put by his side,
Nor the little child that peep'd in at the door, and then drew
  back and was never seen again,

Nor the old man who has lived without purpose, and feels it
    with bitterness worse than gall,
Nor him in the poorhouse tubercled by rum and the bad disorder,
Nor the numberless slaughter'd and wreck'd, nor the brutish
    koboo call'd the ordure of humanity,
Nor the sacs merely floating with open mouths for food to slip in,
Nor any thing in the earth, or down in the oldest graves of the
    earth,
Nor any thing in the myriads of spheres, nor the myriads of
    myriads that inhabit them,
Nor the present, nor the least wisp that is known.

XI

It is time to explain myself — let us stand up.

What is known I strip away,
I launch all men and women forward with me into the Unknown.

The clock indicates the moment — but what does eternity
    indicate ?

We have thus far exhausted trillions of winters and summers,
There are trillions ahead, and trillions ahead of them.

Births have brought us richness and variety,
And other births will bring us richness and variety.

THE BOOK OF HEAVENLY DEATH

I do not call one greater and one smaller,
That which fills its period and place is equal to any.

Were mankind murderous or jealous upon you, my brother, my
    sister?
I am sorry for you, they are not murderous or jealous upon me,
All has been gentle with me, I keep no account with lamentation,
(What have I to do with lamentation?)

I am an acme of things accomplish'd, and I an encloser of
    things to be.

My feet strike an apex of the apices of the stairs,
On every step bunches of ages, and larger bunches between the
    steps,
All below duly travel'd, and still I mount and mount.

Rise after rise bow the phantoms behind me,
Afar down I see the huge first Nothing, I know I was even there,
I waited unseen and always, and slept through the lethargic mist,
And took my time, and took no hurt from the fetid carbon.

Long I was hugg'd close—long and long.

Immense have been the preparations for me,
Faithful and friendly the arms that have help'd me.

Cycles ferried my cradle, rowing and rowing like cheerful
    boatmen,

For room to me stars kept aside in their own rings,
They sent influences to look after what was to hold me.

Before I was born out of my mother generations guided me,
My embryo has never been torpid, nothing could overlay it.

For it the nebula cohered to an orb,
The long slow strata piled to rest it on,
Vast vegetables gave it sustenance,
Monstrous sauroids transported it in their mouths and deposited
    it with care.

All forces have been steadily employ'd to complete and delight me,
Now on this spot I stand with my robust soul.

XII

There is no stoppage and never can be stoppage,
If I, you, and the worlds, and all beneath or upon their surfaces,
    were this moment reduced back to a pallid float, it would
    not avail in the long run,
We should surely bring up again where we now stand,
And surely go as much farther, and then farther and farther.

A few quadrillions of eras, a few octillions of cubic leagues, do not
    hazard the span or make it impatient,
They are but parts, any thing is but a part.

THE BOOK OF HEAVENLY DEATH

See ever so far, there is limitless space outside of that,
Count ever so much, there is limitless time around that.

My rendezvous is appointed, it is certain,
The Lord will be there and wait till I come on perfect terms,
The great Camerado, the lover true for whom I pine will be there.

XIII

I have said that the soul is not more than the body,
And I have said that the body is not more than the soul,
And nothing, not God, is greater to one than one's self is,
And whoever walks a furlong without sympathy walks to his own
    funeral drest in his shroud,
And I or you pocketless of a dime may purchase the pick of the
    earth,
And to glance with an eye or show a bean in its pod confounds
    the learning of all times,
And there is no trade or employment but the young man following
    it may become a hero,
And there is no object so soft but it makes a hub for the wheel'd
    universe,
And I say to any man or woman, Let your soul stand cool and
    composed before a million universes.

And I say to mankind, Be not curious about God,
For I who am curious about each am not curious about God,

THE BOOK OF HEAVENLY DEATH

(No array of terms can say how much I am at peace about God
     and about death.)

I hear and behold God in every object, yet understand God not
     in the least,
Nor do I understand who there can be more wonderful than
     myself.

Why should I wish to see God better than this day?
I see something of God each hour of the twenty-four, and each
     moment then,
In the faces of men and women I see God, and in my own face
     in the glass,
I find letters from God dropt in the street, and every one is sign'd
     by God's name,
And I leave them where they are, for I know that wheresoe'er I go,
Others will punctually come for ever and ever.

And as to you Death, and you bitter hug of mortality, it is idle
     to try to alarm me.

To his work without flinching the accoucheur comes,
I see the elder-hand pressing receiving supporting,
I recline by the sills of the exquisite flexible doors,
And mark the outlet, and mark the relief and escape.

And as to you Corpse I think you are good manure, but that
     does not offend me,

THE BOOK OF HEAVENLY DEATH

I smell the white roses sweet-scented and growing,
I reach to the leafy lips, I reach to the polish'd breasts of melons.

And as to you Life I reckon you are the leavings of many deaths,
(No doubt I have died myself ten thousand times before.)

XIV

There is that in me — I do not know what it is — but I know it
    is in me.

Wrench'd and sweaty — calm and cool then my body becomes,
I sleep — I sleep long.

I do not know it — it is without name — it is a word unsaid,
It is not in any dictionary, utterance, symbol.

Something it swings on more than the earth I swing on,
To it the creation is the friend whose embracing awakes me.

Perhaps I might tell more. Outlines! I plead for my brothers
    and sisters.

Do you see O my brothers and sisters?
It is not chaos or death — it is form, union, plan — it is eternal
    life — it is Happiness.

XV

Death is beautiful from you, (what indeed is finally beautiful
    except death and love?)

THE BOOK OF HEAVENLY DEATH

O I think it is not for life I am chanting here my chant of lovers,
    I think it must be for death,
For how calm, how solemn it grows to ascend to the atmosphere
    of lovers,
Death or life I am then indifferent, my soul declines to prefer,
(I am not sure but the high soul of lovers welcomes death
    most,)
Indeed O death, I think now these leaves mean precisely the
    same as you mean.

XVI

Through me shall the words be said to make death exhilarating,
Give me your tone therefore O death, that I may accord with it,
Give me yourself, for I see that you belong to me now above
    all, and are folded inseparably together, you love and death
    are,
Nor will I allow you to balk me any more with what I was
    calling life,
For now it is convey'd to me that you are the purports essential,
That you hide in these shifting forms of life, for reasons, and
    that they are mainly for you,
That you beyond them come forth to remain, the real reality,
That behind the mask of materials you patiently wait, no matter
    how long,
That you will one day perhaps take control of all,
That you will perhaps dissipate this entire show of appearance,

That may-be you are what it is all for, but it does not last so
    very long,
But you will last very long.

XVII

I see Christ eating the bread of his last supper in the midst of
    youths and old persons,
I see where the strong divine young man the Hercules toil'd
    faithfully and long and then died,
I see the place of the innocent rich life and hapless fate of the
    beautiful nocturnal son, the full-limb'd Bacchus,
I see Kneph, blooming, drest in blue, with the crown of feathers
    on his head,
I see Hermes, unsuspected, dying, well-belov'd, saying to the
    people *Do not weep for me,*
This is not my true country, I have lived banish'd from my true
*   country, I now go back there,*
I return to the celestial sphere where every one goes in his turn.

XVIII

Each of us inevitable,
Each of us limitless — each of us with his or her right upon the
    earth,
Each of us allow'd the eternal purports of the earth,
Each of us here as divinely as any is here.

THE BOOK OF HEAVENLY DEATH

XIX

My spirit has pass'd in compassion and determination around
    the whole earth,
I have look'd for equals and lovers and found them ready for
    me in all lands,
I think some divine rapport has equalized me with them.

XX

All seems beautiful to me,
I can repeat over to men and women You have done such good
    to me I would do the same to you,
I will recruit for myself and you as I go,
I will scatter myself among men and women as I go,
I will toss a new gladness and roughness among them,
Whoever denies me it shall not trouble me,
Whoever accepts me he or she shall be blessed and shall bless me.

XXI

The efflux of the soul,
The efflux of the soul comes from within through embower'd
    gates, ever provoking questions,
These yearnings why are they? these thoughts in the darkness
    why are they?
Why are there men and women that while they are nigh me the
    sunlight expands my blood?

THE BOOK OF HEAVENLY DEATH

Why when they leave me do my pennants of joy sink flat and
    lank?
Why are there trees I never walk under but large and melodious
    thoughts descend upon me?
(I think they hang there winter and summer on those trees and
    always drop fruit as I pass;)
What is it I interchange so suddenly with strangers?
What with some driver as I ride on the seat by his side?
What with some fisherman drawing his seine by the shore as I
    walk by and pause?
What gives me to be free to a woman's and man's good-will?
    what gives them to be free to mine?

The efflux of the soul is happiness, here is happiness,
I think it pervades the open air, waiting at all times,
Now it flows unto us, we are rightly charged.

Allons! whoever you are come travel with me!
Traveling with me you find what never tires.

The earth never tires,
The earth is rude, silent, incomprehensible at first, Nature is
    rude and incomprehensible at first,
Be not discouraged, keep on, there are divine things well
    envelop'd,
I swear to you there are divine things more beautiful than words
    can tell.

XXII

All parts away for the progress of souls,
All religion, all solid things, arts, governments — all that was or
    is apparent upon this globe or any globe, falls into niches
    and corners before the procession of souls along the grand
    roads of the universe.

Of the progress of the souls of men and women along the grand
    roads of the universe, all other progress is the needed
    emblem and sustenance.

Forever alive, forever forward,
Stately, solemn, sad, withdrawn, baffled, mad, turbulent, feeble,
    dissatisfied,
Desperate, proud, fond, sick, accepted by men, rejected by men,
They go! they go! I know that they go, but I know not where
    they go,
But I know that they go toward the best — toward something
    great.

XXIII

Appearances, now or henceforth, indicate what you are,
You necessary film, continue to envelop the soul,
About my body for me, and your body for you, be hung our
    divinest aromas,
Thrive, cities — bring your freight, bring your shows, ample
    and sufficient rivers,

Expand, being than which none else is perhaps more spiritual,
Keep your places, objects than which none else is more lasting.

You have waited, you always wait, you dumb, beautiful ministers,
We receive you with free sense at last, and are insatiate hence-
    forward,
Not you any more shall be able to foil us, or withhold yourselves
    from us,
We use you, and do not cast you aside — we plant you perma-
    nently within us,
We fathom you not—we love you—there is perfection in you also,
You furnish your parts toward eternity,
Great or small, you furnish your parts toward the soul.

XXIV

They prepare for death, yet are they not the finish, but rather
    the outset,
They bring none to his or her terminus or to be content and full,
Whom they take they take into space to behold the birth of
    stars, to learn one of the meanings,
To launch off with absolute faith, to sweep through the cease-
    less rings and never be quiet again.

XXV

O the joy of my soul leaning pois'd on itself, receiving identity
    through materials and loving them, observing characters
    and absorbing them,

My soul vibrated back to me from them, from sight, hearing,
    touch, reason, articulation, comparison, memory, and the
    like,
The real life of my senses and flesh transcending my senses and
    flesh,
My body done with materials, my sight done with my material
    eyes,
Proved to me this day beyond cavil that it is not my material eyes
    which finally see,
Nor my material body which finally loves, walks, laughs, shouts,
    embraces, procreates.

XXVI

Yet O my soul supreme!
Know'st thou the joys of pensive thought?
Joys of the free and lonesome heart, the tender, gloomy heart?
Joys of the solitary walk, the spirit bow'd yet proud, the suffering
    and the struggle?
The agonistic throes, the ecstasies, joys of the solemn musings
    day or night?
Joys of the thought of Death, the great spheres Time and Space?
Prophetic joys of better, loftier love's ideals, the divine wife, the
    sweet, eternal, perfect comrade?
Joys all thine own undying one, joys worthy thee O soul.

THE BOOK OF HEAVENLY DEATH

XXVII

For not life's joys alone I sing, repeating — the joy of death!
The beautiful touch of Death, soothing and benumbing a few
    moments, for reasons,
Myself discharging my excrementitious body to be burn'd, or
    render'd to powder, or buried,
My real body doubtless left to me for other spheres,
My voided body nothing more to me, returning to the purifications,
    further offices, eternal uses of the earth.

XXVIII

Muscle and pluck forever!
What invigorates life invigorates death,
And the dead advance as much as the living advance,
And the future is no more uncertain than the present.

XXIX

How beggarly appear arguments before a defiant deed!
How the floridness of the materials of cities shrivels before a
    man's or woman's look!

All waits or goes by default till a strong being appears;
A strong being is the proof of the race and of the ability of the
    universe,
When he or she appears materials are overaw'd,
The dispute on the soul stops,

The old customs and phrases are confronted, turn'd back, or
    laid away.

What is your money-making now? what can it do now?
What is your respectability now?
What are your theology, tuition, society, traditions, statute-
    books, now?
Where are your jibes of being now?
Where are your cavils about the soul now?

XXX

I say I bring thee Muse to-day and here,
All occupations, duties broad and close,
Toil, healthy toil and sweat, endless, without cessation,
The old, old practical burdens, interests, joys,
The family, parentage, childhood, husband and wife,
The house-comforts, the house itself and all its belongings,
Food and its preservation, chemistry applied to it,
Whatever forms the average, strong, complete, sweet-blooded
    man or woman, the perfect longeve personality,
And helps its present life to health and happiness, and shapes
    its soul,
For the eternal real life to come.

XXXI

Souls of men and women! it is not you I call unseen, unheard,
    untouchable and untouching,

23

It is not you I go argue pro and con about, and to settle whether
you are alive or no,
I own publicly who you are, if nobody else owns.

XXXII

The sun and stars that float in the open air,
The apple-shaped earth and we upon it, surely the drift of them
is something grand,
I do not know what it is except that it is grand, and that it is
happiness,
And that the enclosing purport of us here is not a speculation or
bon-mot or reconnoissance,
And that it is not something which by luck may turn out well for
us, and without luck must be a failure for us,
And not something which may yet be retracted in a certain
contingency.

XXXIII

We consider bibles and religions divine — I do not say they are
not divine,
I say they have all grown out of you, and may grow out of you
still,
It is not they who give the life, it is you who give the life,
Leaves are not more shed from the trees, or trees from the
earth, than they are shed out of you.

THE BOOK OF HEAVENLY DEATH

XXXIV

To her children the words of the eloquent dumb great mother
    never fail,
The true words do not fail, for motion does not fail and reflec-
    tion does not fail,
Also the day and night do not fail, and the voyage we pursue
    does not fail.

XXXV

Tumbling on steadily, nothing dreading,
Sunshine, storm, cold, heat, forever withstanding, passing,
    carrying,
The soul's realization and determination still inheriting,
The fluid vacuum around and ahead still entering and dividing,
No balk retarding, no anchor anchoring, on no rock striking,
Swift, glad, content, unbereav'd, nothing losing,
Of all able and ready at any time to give strict account,
The divine ship sails the divine sea.

Whoever you are! motion and reflection are especially for you,
The divine ship sails the divine sea for you.

Whoever you are! you are he or she for whom the earth is solid
    and liquid,
You are he or she for whom the sun and moon hang in the sky,
For none more than you are the present and the past,
For none more than you is immortality.

THE BOOK OF HEAVENLY DEATH

Each man to himself and each woman to herself, is the word of
    the past and present, and the true word of immortality;
No one can acquire for another — not one,
Not one can grow for another — not one.

The song is to the singer, and comes back most to him,
The teaching is to the teacher, and comes back most to him,
The murder is to the murderer, and comes back most to him,
The theft is to the thief, and comes back most to him,
The love is to the lover, and comes back most to him,
The gift is to the giver, and comes back most to him — it can-
    not fail,
The oration is to the orator, the acting is to the actor and
    actress not to the audience,
And no man understands any greatness or goodness but his
    own, or the indication of his own.

I swear the earth shall surely be complete to him or her who
    shall be complete,
The earth remains jagged and broken only to him or her who
    remains jagged and broken.

I swear there is no greatness or power that does not emulate
    those of the earth,
There can be no theory of any account unless it corroborate the
    theory of the earth,

THE BOOK OF HEAVENLY DEATH

No politics, song, religion, behavior, or what not, is of account,
    unless it compare with the amplitude of the earth,
Unless it face the exactness, vitality, impartiality, rectitude of
    the earth.

I swear I begin to see love with sweeter spasms than that which
    responds love,
It is that which contains itself, which never invites and never
    refuses.

I swear I begin to see little or nothing in audible words,
All merges toward the presentation of the unspoken meanings
    of the earth,
Toward him who sings the songs of the body and of the truths
    of the earth,
Toward him who makes the dictionaries of words that print
    cannot touch.

I swear I see what is better than to tell the best,
It is always to leave the best untold.

When I undertake to tell the best I find I cannot,
My tongue is ineffectual on its pivots,
My breath will not be obedient to its organs,
I become a dumb man.

The best of the earth cannot be told anyhow, all or any is best,
It is not what you anticipated, it is cheaper, easier, nearer,
Things are not dismiss'd from the places they held before,

THE BOOK OF HEAVENLY DEATH

The earth is just as positive and direct as it was before,
Facts, religions, improvements, politics, trades, are as real as
    before,
But the soul is also real, it too is positive and direct,
No reasoning, no proof has establish'd it,
Undeniable growth has establish'd it.

These to echo the tones of souls and the phrases of souls,
(If they did not echo the phrases of souls what were they then?
If they had not reference to you in especial what were they then?)

I swear I will never henceforth have to do with the faith that
    tells the best,
I will have to do only with that faith that leaves the best untold.

Say on, sayers! sing on, singers!
Delve! mould! pile the words of the earth!
Work on, age after age, nothing is to be lost,
It may have to wait long, but it will certainly come in use,
When the materials are all prepared and ready, the architects
    shall appear.

I swear to you the architects shall appear without fail,
I swear to you they will understand you and justify you,
The greatest among them shall be he who best knows you, and
    encloses all and is faithful to all,
He and the rest shall not forget you, they shall perceive that
    you are not an iota less than they,
You shall be fully glorified in them.

THE BOOK OF HEAVENLY DEATH

XXXVI

In this broad earth of ours,
Amid the measureless grossness and the slag,
Enclosed and safe within its central heart,
Nestles the seed perfection.

By every life a share or more or less,
None born but it is born, conceal'd or unconceal'd the seed is
    waiting.

XXXVII

Yet again, lo! the soul, above all science,
For it has history gather'd like husks around the globe,
For it the entire star-myriads roll through the sky.

In spiral routes by long detours,
(As a much-tacking ship upon the sea,)
For it the partial to the permanent flowing,
For it the real to the ideal tends.

For it the mystic evolution,
Not the right only justified, what we call evil also justified.

Forth from their masks, no matter what,
From the huge festering trunk, from craft and guile and tears,
Health to emerge and joy, joy universal.

Out of the bulk, the morbid and the shallow,
Out of the bad majority, the varied countless frauds of men and
    states,

Electric, antiseptic yet, cleaving, suffusing all,
Only the good is universal.

Over the mountain-growths disease and sorrow,
An uncaught bird is ever hovering, hovering,
High in the purer, happier air.

From imperfection's murkiest cloud,
Darts always forth one ray of perfect light,
One flash of heaven's glory.

To fashion's, custom's discord,
To the mad Babel-din, the deafening orgies,
Soothing each lull a strain is heard, just heard,
From some far shore the final chorus sounding.

O the blest eyes, the happy hearts,
That see, that know the guiding thread so fine,
Along the mighty labyrinth.

XXXVIII

All, all for immortality,
Love like the light silently wrapping all,
Nature's amelioration blessing all,
The blossoms, fruits of ages, orchards divine and certain,
Forms, objects, growths, humanities, to spiritual images ripening.

Give me O God to sing that thought,
Give me, give him or her I love this quenchless faith,

THE BOOK OF HEAVENLY DEATH

In Thy ensemble, whatever else withheld withhold not from us,
Belief in plan of Thee enclosed in Time and Space,
Health, peace, salvation universal.

XXXIX

These furies, elements, storms, motions of Nature, throes of
   apparent dissolution, you are he or she who is master or
   mistress over them,
Master or mistress in your own right over Nature, elements,
   pain, passion, dissolution.

XL

O but it is not the years — it is I, it is You,
We touch all laws and tally all antecedents,
We are the skald, the oracle, the monk and the knight, we easily
   include them and more,
We stand amid time beginningless and endless, we stand amid
   evil and good,
All swings around us, there is as much darkness as light,
The very sun swings itself and its system of planets around us,
Its sun, and its again, all swing around us.

XLI

I know that the past was great and the future will be great,
And I know that both curiously conjoint in the present time,

31

THE BOOK OF HEAVENLY DEATH

(For the sake of him I typify, for the common average man's
    sake, your sake if you are he,)
And that where I am or you are this present day, there is the
    centre of all days, all races,
And there is the meaning to us of all that has ever come of
    races and days, or ever will come.

XLII

Whereto answering, the sea,
Delaying not, hurrying not,
Whisper'd me through the night, and very plainly before day-
    break,
Lisp'd to me the low and delicious word death,
And again death, death, death, death,
Hissing melodious, neither like the bird nor like my arous'd
    child's heart,
But edging near as privately for me rustling at my feet,
Creeping thence steadily up to my ears and laving me softly all
    over,
Death, death, death, death, death.

Which I do not forget,
But fuse the song of my dusky demon and brother,
That he sang to me in the moonlight on Paumanok's gray beach,
With the thousand responsive songs at random,
My own songs awaked from that hour,
And with them the key, the word up from the waves,

The word of the sweetest song and all songs,
That strong and delicious word which, creeping to my feet,
(Or like some old crone rocking the cradle, swathed in sweet
    garments, bending aside,)
The sea whisper'd me.

XLIII

Aboard at a ship's helm,
A young steersman steering with care.

Through fog on a sea-coast dolefully ringing,
An ocean-bell — O a warning bell, rock'd by the waves.

O you give good notice indeed, you bell by the sea-reefs ringing,
Ringing, ringing, to warn the ship from its wreck-place.

For as on the alert O steersman, you mind the loud admonition,
The bows turn, the freighted ship tacking speeds away under her
    gray sails,
The beautiful and noble ship with all her precious wealth speeds
    away gayly and safe.

But O the ship, the immortal ship! O ship aboard the ship!
Ship of the body, ship of the soul, voyaging, voyaging, voyaging.

XLIV

On the beach at night,
Stands a child with her father,
Watching the east, the autumn sky.

THE BOOK OF HEAVENLY DEATH

Up through the darkness,
While ravening clouds, the burial clouds, in black masses
    spreading,
Lower sullen and fast athwart and down the sky,
Amid a transparent clear belt of ether yet left in the east,
Ascends large and calm the lord-star Jupiter,
And nigh at hand, only a very little above,
Swim the delicate sisters the Pleiades.

From the beach the child holding the hand of her father,
Those burial-clouds that lower victorious soon to devour all,
Watching, silently weeps.

Weep not, child,
Weep not, my darling,
With these kisses let me remove your tears,
The ravening clouds shall not long be victorious,
They shall not long possess the sky, they devour the stars only
    in apparition,
Jupiter shall emerge, be patient, watch again another night, the
    Pleiades shall emerge,
They are immortal, all those stars both silvery and golden shall
    shine out again,
The great stars and the little ones shall shine out again, they
    endure,
The vast immortal suns and the long-enduring pensive moons
    shall again shine.

THE BOOK OF HEAVENLY DEATH

Then dearest child mournest thou only for Jupiter?
Considerest thou alone the burial of the stars?

Something there is,
(With my lips soothing thee, adding I whisper,
I give thee the first suggestion, the problem and indirection,)
Something there is more immortal even than the stars,
(Many the burials, many the days and nights, passing away,)
Something that shall endure longer even than lustrous Jupiter,
Longer than sun or any revolving satellite,
Or the radiant sisters the Pleiades.

XLV

The world below the brine,
Forests at the bottom of the sea, the branches and leaves,
Sea-lettuce, vast lichens, strange flowers and seeds, the thick
    tangle, openings, and pink turf,
Different colors, pale gray and green, purple, white, and gold,
    the play of light through the water,
Dumb swimmers there among the rocks, coral, gluten, grass,
    rushes, and the aliment of the swimmers,
Sluggish existences grazing there suspended, or slowly crawling
    close to the bottom,
The sperm-whale at the surface blowing air and spray, or
    disporting with his flukes,
The leaden-eyed shark, the walrus, the turtle, the hairy sea-
    leopard, and the sting-ray,

Passions there, wars, pursuits, tribes, sight in those ocean-
    depths, breathing that thick-breathing air, as so many do,
The change thence to the sight here, and to the subtle air
    breathed by beings like us who walk this sphere,
The change onward from ours to that of beings who walk other
    spheres.

XLVI

On the beach at night alone,
As the old mother sways her to and fro singing her husky song,
As I watch the bright stars shining, I think a thought of the
    clef of the universes and of the future.

A vast similitude interlocks all,
All spheres, grown, ungrown, small, large, suns, moons, planets,
All distances of place however wide,
All distances of time, all inanimate forms,
All souls, all living bodies though they be ever so different, or
    in different worlds,
All gaseous, watery, vegetable, mineral processes, the fishes, the
    brutes,
All nations, colors, barbarisms, civilizations, languages,
All identities that have existed or may exist on this globe, or
    any globe,
All lives and deaths, all of the past, present, future,
This vast similitude spans them, and always has spann'd,
And shall forever span them and compactly hold and enclose
    them.

XLVII

Flaunt out O sea your separate flags of nations !
Flaunt out visible as ever the various ship-signals !
But do you reserve especially for yourself and for the soul of
    man one flag above all the rest,
A spiritual woven signal for all nations, emblem of man elate
    above death,
Token of all brave captains and all intrepid sailors and mates,
And all that went down doing their duty,
Reminiscent of them, twined from all intrepid captains young
    or old,
A pennant universal, subtly waving all time, o'er all brave sailors,
All seas, all ships.

XLVIII

O Death, (for Life has served its turn,)
Opener and usher to the heavenly mansion,
Be thou my God.

XLIX

Of ownership—as if one fit to own things could not at pleasure
    enter upon all, and incorporate them into himself or herself ;
Of vista —suppose some sight in arriere through the formative
    chaos, presuming the growth, fulness, life, now attain'd on
    the journey,
(But I see the road continued, and the journey ever continued ;)

THE BOOK OF HEAVENLY DEATH

Of what was once lacking on earth, and in due time has become
    supplied — and of what will yet be supplied,
Because all I see and know I believe to have its main purport
    in what will yet be supplied.

L

When I heard the learn'd astronomer,
When the proofs, the figures, were ranged in columns before me,
When I was shown the charts and diagrams, to add, divide, and
    measure them,
When I sitting heard the astronomer where he lectured with
    much applause in the lecture-room,
How soon unaccountable I became tired and sick,
Till rising and gliding out I wander'd off by myself,
In the mystical moist night-air, and from time to time,
Look'd up in perfect silence at the stars.

LI

Roaming in thought over the Universe, I saw the little that is
    Good steadily hastening towards immortality,
And the vast all that is call'd Evil I saw hastening to merge
    itself and become lost and dead.

LII

Gliding o'er all, through all,
Through Nature, Time, and Space,
As a ship on the waters advancing,

THE BOOK OF HEAVENLY DEATH

The voyage of the soul — not life alone,
Death, many deaths I'll sing.

LIII

Word over all, beautiful as the sky,
Beautiful that war and all its deeds of carnage must in time be
     utterly lost,
That the hands of the sisters Death and Night incessantly softly
     wash again, and ever again, this soil'd world ;
For my enemy is dead, a man divine as myself is dead,
I look where he lies white-faced and still in the coffin — I draw
     near,
Bend down and touch lightly with my lips the white face in the
     coffin.

LIV

(Nor for you, for one alone,
Blossoms and branches green to coffins all I bring,
For fresh as the morning, thus would I chant a song for you O
     sane and sacred death.

All over bouquets of roses,
O death, I cover you over with roses and early lilies,
But mostly and now the lilac that blooms the first,
Copious I break, I break the sprigs from the bushes,
With loaded arms I come, pouring for you,
For you and the coffins all of you O death.)

39

THE BOOK OF HEAVENLY DEATH

LV

Come lovely and soothing death,
Undulate round the world, serenely arriving, arriving,
In the day, in the night, to all, to each,
Sooner or later delicate death.

Prais'd be the fathomless universe,
For life and joy, and for objects and knowledge curious,
And for love, sweet love — but praise ! praise ! praise !
For the sure-enwinding arms of cool-enfolding death.

Dark mother always gliding near with soft feet,
Have none chanted for thee a chant of fullest welcome ?
Then I chant it for thee, I glorify thee above all,
I bring thee a song that when thou must indeed come, come
    unfalteringly.

Approach strong deliveress,
When it is so, when thou hast taken them I joyously sing the dead,
Lost in the loving floating ocean of thee,
Laved in the flood of thy bliss O death.

From me to thee glad serenades,
Dances for thee I propose saluting thee, adornments and feast-
    ings for thee,
And the sights of the open landscape and the high-spread sky
    are fitting,
And life and the fields, and the huge and thoughtful night.

THE BOOK OF HEAVENLY DEATH

The night in silence under many a star,
The ocean shore and the husky whispering wave whose voice I
    know,
And the soul turning to thee O vast and well-veil'd death,
And the body gratefully nestling close to thee.

Over the tree-tops I float thee a song,
Over the rising and sinking waves, over the myriad fields and
    the prairies wide,
Over the dense-pack'd cities all and the teeming wharves and
    ways,
I float this carol with joy, with joy to thee O death.

LVI

Of these States the poet is the equable man,
Not in him but off from him things are grotesque, eccentric,
    fail of their full returns,
Nothing out of its place is good, nothing in its place is bad,
He bestows on every object or quality its fit proportion, neither
    more nor less,
He is the arbiter of the diverse, he is the key,
He is the equalizer of his age and land,
He supplies what wants supplying, he checks what wants
    checking,

In peace out of him speaks the spirit of peace, large, rich,
thrifty, building populous towns, encouraging agriculture,
arts, commerce, lighting the study of man, the soul, health,
immortality, government,

In war he is the best backer of the war, he fetches artillery as
good as the engineer's, he can make every word he speaks
draw blood,

The years straying toward infidelity he withholds by his steady
faith,

He is no arguer, he is judgment, (Nature accepts him absolutely,)

He judges not as the judge judges but as the sun falling round
a helpless thing,

As he sees the farthest he has the most faith,

His thoughts are the hymns of the praise of things,

In the dispute on God and eternity he is silent,

He sees eternity less like a play with a prologue and denouement,

He sees eternity in men and women, he does not see men and
women as dreams or dots.

LVII

Death is without emergencies here, but life is perpetual emergencies here,

Are your body, days, manners, superb? after death you shall
be superb,

Justice, health, self-esteem, clear the way with irresistible power;

How dare you place any thing before a man?

42

LVIII

I will confront these shows of the day and night,
I will know if I am to be less than they,
I will see if I am not as majestic as they,
I will see if I am not as subtle and real as they,
I will see if I am to be less generous than they,
I will see if I have no meaning, while the houses and ships have
     meaning,
I will see if the fishes and birds are to be enough for themselves,
     and I am not to be enough for myself.

I match my spirit against yours you orbs, growths, mountains,
     brutes,
Copious as you are I absorb you all in myself, and become the
     master myself,
America isolated yet embodying all, what is it finally except
     myself?
These States, what are they except myself?

I know now why the earth is gross, tantalizing, wicked, it is for
     my sake,
I take you specially to be mine, you terrible, rude forms.

LIX

Ah the dead to me mar not, they fit well in Nature,
They fit very well in the landscape under the trees and grass,
And along the edge of the sky in the horizon's far margin.

43

THE BOOK OF HEAVENLY DEATH

Nor do I forget you Departed,
Nor in winter or summer my lost ones,
But most in the open air as now when my soul is rapt and at
    peace, like pleasing phantoms,
Your memories rising glide silently by me.

LX

Did we think victory great ?
So it is — but now it seems to me, when it cannot be help'd,
    that defeat is great,
And that death and dismay are great.

LXI

I believe of all those men and women that fill'd the unnamed
    lands, every one exists this hour here or elsewhere, invisible
    to us,
In exact proportion to what he or she grew from in life, and out
    of what he or she did, felt, became, loved, sinn'd, in life.

I believe that was not the end of those nations or any person of
    them, any more than this shall be the end of my nation, or
    of me ;
Of their languages, governments, marriage, literature, products,
    games, wars, manners, crimes, prisons, slaves, heroes,
    poets,

I suspect their results curiously await in the yet unseen world,
    counterparts of what accrued to them in the seen world,
I suspect I shall meet them there,
I suspect I shall there find each old particular of those unnamed
    lands.

LXII

The soul is of itself,
All verges to it, all has reference to what ensues,
All that a person does, says, thinks, is of consequence,
Not a move can a man or woman make, that affects him or her
    in a day, month, any part of the direct lifetime, or the hour
    of death,
But the same affects him or her onward afterward through the
    indirect lifetime.

The indirect is just as much as the direct,
The spirit receives from the body just as much as it gives to the
    body, if not more.

Not one word or deed, not venereal sore, discoloration, privacy
    of the onanist,
Putridity of gluttons or rum-drinkers, peculation, cunning,
    betrayal, murder, seduction, prostitution,
But has results beyond death as really as before death.

THE BOOK OF HEAVENLY DEATH

LXIII

Singly, wholly, to affect now, affected their time, will forever
    affect, all of the past and all of the present and all of the
    future,

All the brave actions of war and peace,

All help given to relatives, strangers, the poor, old, sorrowful,
    young children, widows, the sick, and to shunn'd persons,

All self-denial that stood steady and aloof on wrecks, and saw
    others fill the seats of the boats,

All offering of substance or life for the good old cause, or for a
    friend's sake, or opinion's sake,

All pains of enthusiasts scoff'd at by their neighbors,

All the limitless sweet love and precious suffering of mothers,

All honest men baffled in strifes recorded or unrecorded,

All the grandeur and good of ancient nations whose fragments
    we inherit,

All the good of the dozens of ancient nations unknown to us by
    name, date, location,

All that was ever manfully begun, whether it succeeded or no,

All suggestions of the divine mind of man or the divinity of his
    mouth, or the shaping of his great hands,

All that is well thought or said this day on any part of the globe,
    or on any of the wandering stars, or on any of the fix'd
    stars, by those there as we are here,

All that is henceforth to be thought or done by you whoever you
    are, or by any one,

These inure, have inured, shall inure, to the identities from which
    they sprang, or shall spring.

LXIV

Did you guess any thing lived only its moment?
The world does not so exist, no parts palpable or impalpable so
    exist,
No consummation exists without being from some long previous
    consummation, and that from some other,
Without the farthest conceivable one coming a bit nearer the
    beginning than any.

Whatever satisfies souls is true;
Prudence entirely satisfies the craving and glut of souls,
Itself only finally satisfies the soul,
The soul has that measureless pride which revolts from every
    lesson but its own.

Now I breathe the word of the prudence that walks abreast with
    time, space, reality,
That answers the pride which refuses every lesson but its own.

What is prudence is indivisible,
Declines to separate one part of life from every part,
Divides not the righteous from the unrighteous or the living
    from the dead,
Matches every thought or act by its correlative,

47

Knows no possible forgiveness or deputed atonement,

Knows that the young man who composedly peril'd his life and
lost it has done exceedingly well for himself without doubt,

That he who never peril'd his life, but retains it to old age in
riches and ease, has probably achiev'd nothing for himself
worth mentioning,

Knows that only that person has really learn'd who has learn'd
to prefer results,

Who favors body and soul the same,

Who perceives the indirect assuredly following the direct,

Who in his spirit in any emergency whatever neither hurries
nor avoids death.

LXV

I lie abstracted and hear beautiful tales of things and the
reasons of things,

They are so beautiful I nudge myself to listen.

I cannot say to any person what I hear — I cannot say it to
myself — it is very wonderful.

It is no small matter, this round and delicious globe moving so
exactly in its orbit for ever and ever, without one jolt or the
untruth of a single second,

I do not think it was made in six days, nor in ten thousand
years, nor ten billions of years,

Nor plann'd and built one thing after another as an architect
plans and builds a house.

I do not think seventy years is the time of a man or woman,
Nor that seventy millions of years is the time of a man or woman,
Nor that years will ever stop the existence of me, or any one else.

Is it wonderful that I should be immortal? as every one is immortal;
I know it is wonderful, but my eyesight is equally wonderful,
and how I was conceived in my mother's womb is equally
wonderful,
And pass'd from a babe in the creeping trance of a couple of
summers and winters to articulate and walk—all this is
equally wonderful.

And that my soul embraces you this hour, and we affect each
other without ever seeing each other, and never perhaps to
see each other, is every bit as wonderful.

And that I can think such thoughts as these is just as wonderful,
And that I can remind you, and you think them and know them
to be true, is just as wonderful.

And that the moon spins round the earth and on with the earth,
is equally wonderful,
And that they balance themselves with the sun and stars is
equally wonderful.

THE BOOK OF HEAVENLY DEATH

LXVI

And I said, moreover,
Haply what thou hast heard O soul was not the sound of winds,
Nor dream of raging storm, nor sea-hawk's flapping wings nor
    harsh scream,
Nor vocalism of sun-bright Italy,
Nor German organ majestic, nor vast concourse of voices, nor
    layers of harmonies,
Nor strophes of husbands and wives, nor sound of marching
    soldiers,
Nor flutes, nor harps, nor the bugle-calls of camps,
But to a new rhythmus fitted for thee,
Poems bridging the way from Life to Death, vaguely wafted in
    night air, uncaught, unwritten,
Which let us go forth in the bold day and write.

LXVII

Passage to India!
Lo, soul, seest thou not God's purpose from the first?
The earth to be spann'd, connected by network,
The races, neighbors, to marry and be given in marriage,
The oceans to be cross'd, the distant brought near,
The lands to be welded together.

A worship new I sing,
You captains, voyagers, explorers, yours,

THE BOOK OF HEAVENLY DEATH

You engineers, you architects, machinists, yours,
You, not for trade or transportation only,
But in God's name, and for thy sake O soul.

LXVIII

O vast Rondure, swimming in space,
Cover'd all over with visible power and beauty,
Alternate light and day and the teeming spiritual darkness,
Unspeakable high processions of sun and moon and countless
    stars above,
Below, the manifold grass and waters, animals, mountains, trees,
With inscrutable purpose, some hidden prophetic intention,
Now first it seems my thought begins to span thee.

Down from the gardens of Asia descending radiating,
Adam and Eve appear, then their myriad progeny after them,
Wandering, yearning, curious, with restless explorations,
With questionings, baffled, formless, feverish, with never-happy
    hearts,
With that sad incessant refrain, *Wherefore unsatisfied soul?* and
    Whither O mocking life?

Ah who shall soothe these feverish children?
Who justify these restless explorations?
Who speak the secret of impassive earth?
Who bind it to us? what is this separate Nature so unnatural?

THE BOOK OF HEAVENLY DEATH

What is this earth to our affections? (unloving earth, without a
    throb to answer ours,
Cold earth, the place of graves.)

Yet soul be sure the first intent remains, and shall be carried out,
Perhaps even now the time has arrived.

After the seas are all cross'd, (as they seem already cross'd,)
After the great captains and engineers have accomplish'd their
    work,
After the noble inventors, after the scientists, the chemist, the
    geologist, ethnologist,
Finally shall come the poet worthy that name,
The true son of God shall come singing his songs.

Then not your deeds only O voyagers, O scientists and inventors,
    shall be justified,
All these hearts as of fretted children shall be sooth'd,
All affection shall be fully responded to, the secret shall be told,
All these separations and gaps shall be taken up and hook'd
    and link'd together,
The whole earth, this cold, impassive, voiceless earth, shall be
    completely justified,
Trinitas divine shall be gloriously accomplish'd and compacted
    by the true son of God, the poet,
(He shall indeed pass the straits and conquer the mountains,
He shall double the cape of Good Hope to some purpose,)

THE BOOK OF HEAVENLY DEATH

Nature and Man shall be disjoin'd and diffused no more,
The true son of God shall absolutely fuse them.

LXIX

O we can wait no longer,
We too take ship O soul,
Joyous we too launch out on trackless seas,
Fearless for unknown shores on waves of ecstasy to sail,
Amid the wafting winds, (thou pressing me to thee, I thee to me,
    O soul,)
Caroling free, singing our song of God,
Chanting our chant of pleasant exploration.

With laugh and many a kiss,
(Let others deprecate, let others weep for sin, remorse, humilia-
    tion,)
O soul thou pleasest me, I thee.

Ah more than any priest O soul we too believe in God,
But with the mystery of God we dare not dally.

O soul thou pleasest me, I thee,
Sailing these seas or on the hills, or waking in the night,
Thoughts, silent thoughts, of Time and Space and Death, like
    waters flowing,
Bear me indeed as through the regions infinite,
Whose air I breathe, whose ripples hear, lave me all over,

THE BOOK OF HEAVENLY DEATH

Bathe me O God in thee, mounting to thee,
I and my soul to range in range of thee.

O Thou transcendent,
Nameless, the fibre and the breath,
Light of the light, shedding forth universes, thou centre of them,
Thou mightier centre of the true, the good, the loving,
Thou moral, spiritual fountain — affection's source — thou res-
    ervoir,
(O pensive soul of me — O thirst unsatisfied — waitest not there ?
Waitest not haply for us somewhere there the Comrade perfect ?)
Thou pulse — thou motive of the stars, suns, systems,
That, circling, move in order, safe, harmonious,
Athwart the shapeless vastnesses of space,
How should I think, how breathe a single breath, how speak, if,
    out of myself,
I could not launch, to those, superior universes ?

Swiftly I shrivel at the thought of God,
At Nature and its wonders, Time and Space and Death,
But that I, turning, call to thee O soul, thou actual Me,
And lo, thou gently masterest the orbs,
Thou matest Time, smilest content at Death,
And fillest, swellest full the vastnesses of Space.

Greater than stars or suns,
Bounding O soul thou journeyest forth ;

THE BOOK OF HEAVENLY DEATH

What love than thine and ours could wider amplify?
What aspirations, wishes, outvie thine and ours O soul?
What dreams of the ideal? what plans of purity, perfection,
    strength?
What cheerful willingness for others' sake to give up all?
For others' sake to suffer all?

Reckoning ahead O soul, when thou, the time achiev'd,
The seas all cross'd, weather'd the capes, the voyage done,
Surrounded, copest, frontest God, yieldest, the aim attain'd,
As fill'd with friendship, love complete, the Elder Brother found,
The Younger melts in fondness in his arms.

Passage to more than India!
Are thy wings plumed indeed for such far flights?
O soul, voyagest thou indeed on voyages like those?
Disportest thou on waters such as those?
Soundest below the Sanscrit and the Vedas?
Then have thy bent unleash'd.

Passage to you, your shores, ye aged fierce enigmas!
Passage to you, to mastership of you, ye strangling problems!
You, strew'd with the wrecks of skeletons, that, living, never
    reach'd you.

Passage to more than India!
O secret of the earth and sky!
Of you O waters of the sea! O winding creeks and rivers!

THE BOOK OF HEAVENLY DEATH

Of you O woods and fields! of you strong mountains of my
    land!
Of you O prairies! of you gray rocks!
O morning red! O clouds! O rain and snows!
O day and night, passage to you!

O sun and moon and all you stars! Sirius and Jupiter!
Passage to you!

Passage, immediate passage! the blood burns in my veins!
Away O soul! hoist instantly the anchor!
Cut the hawsers — haul out — shake out every sail!
Have we not stood here like trees in the ground long enough?
Have we not grovel'd here long enough, eating and drinking
    like mere brutes?
Have we not darken'd and dazed ourselves with books long
    enough?

Sail forth — steer for the deep waters only,
Reckless O soul, exploring, I with thee, and thou with me,
For we are bound where mariner has not yet dared to go,
And we will risk the ship, ourselves and all.

O my brave soul!
O farther farther sail!
O daring joy, but safe! are they not all the seas of God?
O farther, farther, farther sail!

THE BOOK OF HEAVENLY DEATH

LXX

Thou O God my life hast lighted,
With ray of light, steady, ineffable, vouchsafed of Thee,
Light rare untellable, lighting the very light,
Beyond all signs, descriptions, languages ;
For that O God, be it my latest word, here on my knees,
Old, poor, and paralyzed, I thank Thee.

My terminus near,
The clouds already closing in upon me,
The voyage balk'd, the course disputed, lost,
I yield my ships to Thee.

My hands, my limbs grow nerveless,
My brain feels rack'd, bewilder'd,
Let the old timbers part, I will not part,
I will cling fast to Thee, O God, though the waves buffet me,
Thee, Thee at least I know.

LXXI

And these things I see suddenly, what mean they ?
As if some miracle, some hand divine unseal'd my eyes,
Shadowy vast shapes smile through the air and sky,
And on the distant waves sail countless ships,
And anthems in new tongues I hear saluting me.

THE BOOK OF HEAVENLY DEATH

LXXII

Peace is always beautiful,
The myth of heaven indicates peace and night.

The myth of heaven indicates the soul,
The soul is always beautiful, it appears more or it appears less,
it comes or it lags behind,
It comes from its embower'd garden and looks pleasantly on
itself and encloses the world,
Perfect and clean the genitals previously jetting, and perfect and
clean the womb cohering,
The head well-grown proportion'd and plumb, and the bowels
and joints porportion'd and plumb.

The soul is always beautiful,
The universe is duly in order, every thing is in its place,
What has arrived is in its place and what waits shall be in its place,
The twisted skull waits, the watery or rotten blood waits,
The child of the glutton or venerealee waits long, and the child
of the drunkard waits long, and the drunkard himself waits
long,
The sleepers that lived and died wait, the far advanced are to
go on in their turns, and the far behind are to come on in
their turns,
The diverse shall be no less diverse, but they shall flow and
unite — they unite now.

58

THE BOOK OF HEAVENLY DEATH

LXXIII

I too pass from the night,
I stay a while away O night, but I return to you again and love you.

Why should I be afraid to trust myself to you?
I am not afraid, I have been well brought forward by you,
I love the rich running day, but I do not desert her in whom I
    lay so long,
I know not how I came of you and I know not where I go with
    you, but I know I came well and shall go well.

I will stop only a time with the night, and rise betimes,
I will duly pass the day O my mother, and duly return to you.

LXXIV

Have you guess'd you yourself would not continue?
Have you dreaded these earth-beetles?
Have you fear'd the future would be nothing to you?

Is to-day nothing? is the beginningless past nothing?
If the future is nothing they are just as surely nothing.

To think that the sun rose in the east — that men and women
    were flexible, real, alive — that every thing was alive,
To think that you and I did not see, feel, think, nor bear our part,
To think that we are now here and bear our part.

THE BOOK OF HEAVENLY DEATH

LXXV

The corpse stretches on the bed and the living look upon it,
It is palpable as the living are palpable.

The living look upon the corpse with their eyesight,
But without eyesight lingers a different living and looks curiously
    on the corpse.

LXXVI

(I see one building the house that serves him a few years, or
    seventy or eighty years at most,
I see one building the house that serves him longer than that.)

LXXVII

What will be will be well, for what is is well,
To take interest is well, and not to take interest shall be well.

LXXVIII

The earth is not an echo, man and his life and all the things of
    his life are well-consider'd.

You are not thrown to the winds, you gather certainly and safely
    around yourself,
Yourself! yourself! yourself, for ever and ever!

THE BOOK OF HEAVENLY DEATH

It is not to diffuse you that you were born of your mother and
    father, it is to identify you,
It is not that you should be undecided, but that you should be
    decided,
Something long preparing and formless is arrived and form'd
    in you,
You are henceforth secure, whatever comes or goes.

The threads that were spun are gather'd, the weft crosses the
    warp, the pattern is systematic.

The preparations have every one been justified,
The orchestra have sufficiently tuned their instruments, the baton
    has given the signal.

The guest that was coming, he waited long, he is now housed,
He is one of those who are beautiful and happy, he is one of
    those that to look upon and be with is enough.

LXXIX

And I have dream'd that the purpose and essence of the known
    life, the transient,
Is to form and decide identity for the unknown life, the
    permanent.

If all came but to ashes of dung,
If maggots and rats ended us, then Alarum! for we are betray'd,
Then indeed suspicion of death.

THE BOOK OF HEAVENLY DEATH

Do you suspect death? if I were to suspect death I should die
    now,
Do you think I could walk pleasantly and well-suited toward
    annihilation?

Pleasantly and well-suited I walk,
Whither I walk I cannot define, but I know it is good,
The whole universe indicates that it is good,
The past and the present indicate that it is good.

How beautiful and perfect are the animals!
How perfect the earth, and the minutest thing upon it!
What is called good is perfect, and what is called bad is just as
    perfect,
The vegetables and minerals are all perfect, and the imponder-
    able fluids perfect;
Slowly and surely they have pass'd on to this, and slowly and
    surely they yet pass on.

I swear I think now that every thing without exception has an
    eternal soul!
The trees have, rooted in the ground! the weeds of the sea
    have! the animals!

I swear I think there is nothing but immortality!
That the exquisite scheme is for it, and the nebulous float is for
    it, and the cohering is for it!

THE BOOK OF HEAVENLY DEATH

And all preparation is for it — and identity is for it — and life
    and materials are altogether for it!

LXXX

Darest thou now O soul,
Walk out with me toward the unknown region,
Where neither ground is for the feet nor any path to follow?

No map there, nor guide,
Nor voice sounding, nor touch of human hand,
Nor face with blooming flesh, nor lips, nor eyes, are in that land.

I know it not O soul,
Nor dost thou, all is a blank before us,
All waits undream'd of in that region, that inaccessible land.

Till when the ties loosen,
All but the ties eternal, Time and Space,
Nor darkness, gravitation, sense, nor any bounds bounding us.

Then we burst forth, we float,
In Time and Space O soul, prepared for them,
Equal, equipt at last, (O joy! O fruit of all!) them to fulfil O
    soul.

LXXXI

Whispers of heavenly death murmur'd I hear,
Labial gossip of night, sibilant chorals,

63

THE BOOK OF HEAVENLY DEATH

Footsteps gently ascending, mystical breezes wafted soft and low,
Ripples of unseen rivers, tides of a current flowing, forever
    flowing,
(Or is it the plashing of tears? the measureless waters of human
    tears?)

I see, just see skyward, great cloud-masses,
Mournfully slowly they roll, silently swelling and mixing,
With at times a half-dimm'd sadden'd far-off star,
Appearing and disappearing.

(Some parturition rather, some solemn immortal birth,
On the frontiers to eyes impenetrable,
Some soul is passing over.)

LXXXII

Chanting the square deific, out of the One advancing, out of the
    sides,
Out of the old and new, out of the square entirely divine,
Solid, four-sided, (all the sides needed,) from this side Jehovah
    am I,
Old Brahm I, and I Saturnius am;
Not Time affects me — I am Time, old, modern as any,
Unpersuadable, relentless, executing righteous judgments,
As the Earth, the Father, the brown old Kronos, with laws,

THE BOOK OF HEAVENLY DEATH

Aged beyond computation, yet ever new, ever with those mighty
    laws rolling,
Relentless I forgive no man — whoever sins dies — I will have
    that man's life ;
Therefore let none expect mercy — have the seasons, gravitation,
    the appointed days, mercy ? no more have I,
But as the seasons and gravitation, and as all the appointed days
    that forgive not,
I dispense from this side judgments inexorable without the least
    remorse.

Consolator most mild, the promis'd one advancing,
With gentle hand extended, the mightier God am I,
Foretold by prophets and poets in their most rapt prophecies and
    poems,
From this side, lo ! the Lord Christ gazes — lo ! Hermes I — lo !
    mine is Hercules' face,
All sorrow, labor, suffering, I, tallying it, absorb in myself,
Many times have I been rejected, taunted, put in prison, and
    crucified, and many times shall be again,
All the world have I given up for my dear brothers' and sisters'
    sake, for the soul's sake,
Wending my way through the homes of men, rich or poor, with
    the kiss of affection,
For I am affection, I am the cheer-bringing God, with hope and
    all-enclosing charity,

THE BOOK OF HEAVENLY DEATH

With indulgent words as to children, with fresh and sane words,
  mine only,
Young and strong I pass knowing well I am destin'd myself to
  an early death ;
But my charity has no death — my wisdom dies not, neither
  early nor late,
And my sweet love bequeath'd here and elsewhere never dies.

Aloof, dissatisfied, plotting revolt,
Comrade of criminals, brother of slaves,
Crafty, despised, a drudge, ignorant,
With sudra face and worn brow, black, but in the depths of my
  heart, proud as any,
Lifted now and always against whoever scorning assumes to rule
  me,
Morose, full of guile, full of reminiscences, brooding, with many
  wiles,
(Though it was thought I was baffled and dispel'd, and my wiles
  done, but that will never be,)
Defiant, I, Satan, still live, still utter words, in new lands duly
  appearing, (and old ones also,)
Permanent here from my side, warlike, equal with any, real as
  any,
Nor time nor change shall ever change me or my words.

Santa Spirita, breather, life,
Beyond the light, lighter than light,

THE BOOK OF HEAVENLY DEATH

Beyond the flames of hell, joyous, leaping easily above hell,
Beyond Paradise, perfumed solely with mine own perfume,
Including all life on earth, touching, including God, including
    Saviour and Satan,
Ethereal, pervading all, (for without me what were all? what
    were God?)
Essence of forms, life of the real identities, permanent, positive,
    (namely the unseen,)
Life of the great round world, the sun and stars, and of man, I,
    the general soul,
Here the square finishing, the solid, I the most solid,
Breathe my breath also through these songs.

LXXXIII

Of him I love day and night I dream'd I heard he was dead,
And I dream'd I went where they had buried him I love, but he
    was not in that place,
And I dream'd I wander'd searching among burial-places to find
    him,
And I found that every place was a burial-place;
The houses full of life were equally full of death, (this house is
    now,)
The streets, the shipping, the places of amusement, the Chicago,
    Boston, Philadelphia, the Mannahatta, were as full of the
    dead as of the living,
And fuller, O vastly fuller of the dead than of the living;

THE BOOK OF HEAVENLY DEATH

And what I dream'd I will henceforth tell to every person and age,
And I stand henceforth bound to what I dream'd,
And now I am willing to disregard burial-places and dispense
    with them,
And if the memorials of the dead were put up indifferently every-
    where, even in the room where I eat or sleep, I should be
    satisfied,
And if the corpse of any one I love, or if my own corpse, be
    duly render'd to powder and pour'd in the sea, I shall
    be satisfied,
Or if it be distributed to the winds I shall be satisfied.

LXXXIV

Yet, yet, ye downcast hours, I know ye also,
Weights of lead, how ye clog and cling at my ankles,
Earth to a chamber of mourning turns — I hear the o'erweening,
    mocking voice,
Matter is conqueror — matter, triumphant only, continues onward.

Despairing cries float ceaselessly toward me,
The call of my nearest lover, putting forth, alarm'd, uncertain,
The sea I am quickly to sail, come tell me,
Come tell me where I am speeding, tell me my destination.

I understand your anguish, but I cannot help you,
I approach, hear, behold, the sad mouth, the look out of the eyes,
    your mute inquiry,

Whither I go from the bed I recline on, come tell me;
Old age, alarm'd, uncertain — a young woman's voice, appealing
to me for comfort;
A young man's voice, *Shall I not escape?*

LXXXV

As if a phantom caress'd me,
I thought I was not alone walking here by the shore;
But the one I thought was with me as now I walk by the shore,
the one I loved that caress'd me,
As I lean and look through the glimmering light, that one has
utterly disappear'd,
And those appear that are hateful to me and mock me.

LXXXVI

I need no assurances, I am a man who is pre-occupied of his
own soul;
I do not doubt that from under the feet and beside the hands
and face I am cognizant of, are now looking faces I am not
cognizant of, calm and actual faces,
I do not doubt but the majesty and beauty of the world are latent
in any iota of the world,
I do not doubt I am limitless, and that the universes are limitless,
in vain I try to think how limitless,

69

I do not doubt that the orbs and the systems of orbs play their
swift sports through the air on purpose, and that I shall one
day be eligible to do as much as they, and more than they,

I do not doubt that temporary affairs keep on and on millions of
years,

I do not doubt interiors have their interiors, and exteriors have
their exteriors, and that the eyesight has another eyesight,
and the hearing another hearing, and the voice another
voice,

I do not doubt that the passionately-wept deaths of young men
are provided for, and that the deaths of young women and
the deaths of little children are provided for,

(Did you think Life was so well provided for, and Death, the purport of all Life, is not well provided for?)

I do not doubt that wrecks at sea, no matter what the horrors of
them, no matter whose wife, child, husband, father, lover,
has gone down, are provided for, to the minutest points,

I do not doubt that whatever can possibly happen anywhere at
any time, is provided for in the inherences of things,

I do not think Life provides for all and for Time and Space, but
I believe Heavenly Death provides for all.

LXXXVII

Quicksand years that whirl me I know not whither,

Your schemes, politics, fail, lines give way, substances mock and
elude me,

Only the theme I sing, the great and strong-possess'd soul, eludes
  not,
One's-self must never give way — that is the final substance —
  that out of all is sure,
Out of politics, triumphs, battles, life, what at last finally remains ?
When shows break up what but One's-Self is sure ?

LXXXVIII

That music always round me, unceasing, unbeginning, yet long
  untaught I did not hear,
But now the chorus I hear and am elated,
A tenor, strong, ascending with power and health, with glad notes
  of daybreak I hear,
A soprano at intervals sailing buoyantly over the tops of immense
  waves,
A transparent base shuddering lusciously under and through the
  universe,
The triumphant tutti, the funeral wailings with sweet flutes and
  violins, all these I fill myself with,
I hear not the volumes of sound merely, I am moved by the
  exquisite meanings,
I listen to the different voices winding in and out, striving, con-
  tending with fiery vehemence to excel each other in emotion ;
I do not think the performers know themselves — but now I think
  I begin to know them.

THE BOOK OF HEAVENLY DEATH

LXXXIX

What ship puzzled at sea, cons for the true reckoning?
Or coming in, to avoid the bars and follow the channel a perfect
    pilot needs?
Here, sailor! here, ship! take aboard the most perfect pilot,
Whom, in a little boat, putting off and rowing, I hailing you offer.

XC

A noiseless patient spider,
I mark'd where on a little promontory it stood isolated,
Mark'd how to explore the vacant vast surrounding,
It launch'd forth filament, filament, filament, out of itself,
Ever unreeling them, ever tirelessly speeding them.

And you O my soul where you stand,
Surrounded, detached, in measureless oceans of space,
Ceaselessly musing, venturing, throwing, seeking the spheres to
    connect them,
Till the bridge you will need be form'd, till the ductile anchor
    hold,
Till the gossamer thread you fling catch somewhere, O my soul.

XCI

O living always, always dying!
O the burials of me past and present,

THE BOOK OF HEAVENLY DEATH

O me while I stride ahead, material, visible, imperious as ever;
O me, what I was for years, now dead, (I lament not, I am
    content;)
O to disengage myself from those corpses of me, which I turn
    and look at where I cast them,
To pass on, (O living! always living!) and leave the corpses
    behind.

XCII

From all the rest I single out you, having a message for you,
You are to die — let others tell you what they please, I cannot
    prevaricate,
I am exact and merciless, but I love you — there is no escape
    for you.

Softly I lay my right hand upon you, you just feel it,
I do not argue, I bend my head close and half envelop it,
I sit quietly by, I remain faithful,
I am more than nurse, more than parent or neighbor,
I absolve you from all except yourself spiritual bodily, that is
    eternal, you yourself will surely escape,
The corpse you will leave will be but excrementitious.

The sun bursts through in unlooked-for directions,
Strong thoughts fill you and confidence, you smile,
You forget you are sick, as I forget you are sick,

You do not see the medicines, you do not mind the weeping
    friends, I am with you,
I exclude others from you, there is nothing to be commiserated,
I do not commiserate, I congratulate you.

XCIII

Night on the prairies,
The supper is over, the fire on the ground burns low,
The wearied emigrants sleep, wrapt in their blankets;
I walk by myself — I stand and look at the stars, which I think
    now I never realized before.

Now I absorb immortality and peace,
I admire death and test propositions.

How plenteous! how spiritual! how resumé!
The same old man and soul — the same old aspirations, and
    the same content.

I was thinking the day most splendid till I saw what the not-day
    exhibited,
I was thinking this globe enough till there sprang out so noiseless
    around me myriads of other globes.

Now while the great thoughts of space and eternity fill me I will
    measure myself by them,
And now touch'd with the lives of other globes arrived as far
    along as those of the earth,

Or waiting to arrive, or pass'd on farther than those of the earth,
I henceforth no more ignore them than I ignore my own life,
Or the lives of the earth arrived as far as mine, or waiting to
    arrive.

O I see now that life cannot exhibit all to me, as the day cannot,
I see that I am to wait for what will be exhibited by death.

XCIV

As I sit with others at a great feast, suddenly while the music is
    playing,
To my mind, (whence it comes I know not,) spectral in mist of
    a wreck at sea,
Of certain ships, how they sail from port with flying streamers
    and wafted kisses, and that is the last of them,
Of the solemn and murky mystery about the fate of the President,
Of the flower of the marine science of fifty generations founder'd
    off the Northeast coast and going down — of the steamship
    Arctic going down,
Of the veil'd tableau — women gather'd together on deck, pale,
    heroic, waiting the moment that draws so close — O the
    moment!
A huge sob — a few bubbles — the white foam spirting up —
    and then the women gone,
Sinking there while the passionless wet flows on — and I now
    pondering, Are those women indeed gone?

THE BOOK OF HEAVENLY DEATH

Are souls drown'd and destroy'd so?
Is only matter triumphant?

XCV

At the last, tenderly,
From the walls of the powerful fortress'd house,
From the clasp of the knitted locks, from the keep of the well-
    closed doors,
Let me be wafted.

Let me glide noiselessly forth;
With the key of softness unlock the locks — with a whisper,
Set ope the doors O soul.

Tenderly — be not impatient,
(Strong is your hold O mortal flesh,
Strong is your hold O love.)

XCVI

As I watch'd the ploughman ploughing,
Or the sower sowing in the fields, or the harvester harvesting,
I saw there too, O life and death, your analogies;
(Life, life is the tillage, and Death is the harvest according.)

XCVII

Pensive and faltering,
The words *the Dead* I write,

THE BOOK OF HEAVENLY DEATH

For living are the Dead,
(Haply the only living, only real,
And I the apparition, I the spectre.)

XCVIII

The soul, its destinies, the real real,
(Purport of all these apparitions of the real;)
In thee America, the soul, its destinies,
Thou globe of globes ! thou wonder nebulous !
By many a throe of heat and cold convuls'd, (by these thyself
    solidifying,)
Thou mental, moral orb — thou New, indeed new, Spiritual
    World !
The Present holds thee not — for such vast growth as thine,
For such unparallel'd flight as thine, such brood as thine,
The FUTURE only holds thee and can hold thee.

XCIX

I saw the face of the most smear'd and slobbering idiot they had
    at the asylum,
And I knew for my consolation what they knew not,
I knew of the agents that emptied and broke my brother,
The same wait to clear the rubbish from the fallen tenement,
And I shall look again in a score or two of ages,
And I shall meet the real landlord perfect and unharm'd, every
    inch as good as myself.

THE BOOK OF HEAVENLY DEATH

The Lord advances, and yet advances,
Always the shadow in front, always the reach'd hand bringing
　　up the laggards.

Out of this face emerge banners and horses — O superb! I see
　　what is coming,
I see the high pioneer-caps, see staves of runners clearing the
　　way,
I hear victorious drums.

This face is a life-boat,
This is the face commanding and bearded, it asks no odds of the
　　rest,
This face is flavor'd fruit ready for eating,
This face of a healthy honest boy is the programme of all good.

These faces bear testimony slumbering or awake,
They show their descent from the Master himself.

Off the word I have spoken I except not one — red, white, black,
　　are all deific,
In each house is the ovum, it comes forth after a thousand years.

Spots or cracks at the windows do not disturb me,
Tall and sufficient stand behind and make signs to me,
I read the promise and patiently wait.

THE BOOK OF HEAVENLY DEATH

C

Blow trumpeter free and clear, I follow thee,
While at thy liquid prelude, glad, serene,
The fretting world, the streets, the noisy hours of day withdraw,
A holy calm descends like dew upon me,
I walk in cool refreshing night the walks of Paradise,
I scent the grass, the moist air and the roses;
Thy song expands my numb'd imbonded spirit, thou freest,
    launchest me,
Floating and basking upon heaven's lake.

CI

O how the immortal phantoms crowd around me!
I see the vast alembic ever working, I see and know the flames
    that heat the world,
The glow, the blush, the beating hearts of lovers,
So blissful happy some, and some so silent, dark, and nigh to
    death;
Love, that is all the earth to lovers—love, that mocks time and
    space,
Love, that is day and night—love, that is sun and moon and
    stars,
Love, that is crimson, sumptuous, sick with perfume,
No other words but words of love, no other thought but love.

79

CII

Now trumpeter for thy close,
Vouchsafe a higher strain than any yet,
Sing to my soul, renew its languishing faith and hope,
Rouse up my slow belief, give me some vision of the future,
Give me for once its prophecy and joy.

O glad, exulting, culminating song!
A vigor more than earth's is in thy notes,
Marches of victory — man disenthral'd — the conqueror at last,
Hymns to the universal God from universal man — all joy!
A reborn race appears — a perfect world, all joy!
Women and men in wisdom innocence and health — all joy!
Riotous laughing bacchanals fill'd with joy!
War, sorrow, suffering gone — the rank earth purged — nothing
    but joy left!
The ocean fill'd with joy — the atmosphere all joy!
Joy! joy! in freedom, worship, love! joy in the ecstasy of life!
Enough to merely be! enough to breathe!
Joy! joy! all over joy!

CIII

O me, man of slack faith so long,
Standing aloof, denying portions so long,
Only aware to-day of compact all-diffused truth,

THE BOOK OF HEAVENLY DEATH

Discovering to-day there is no lie or form of lie, and can be
    none, but grows as inevitably upon itself as the truth does
    upon itself,
Or as any law of the earth or any natural production of the
    earth does.

(This is curious and may not be realized immediately, but it
    must be realized,
I feel in myself that I represent falsehoods equally with the rest,
And that the universe does.)

Where has fail'd a perfect return indifferent of lies or the truth?
Is it upon the ground, or in water or fire? or in the spirit of
    man? or in the meat and blood?

Meditating among liars and retreating sternly into myself, I see
    that there are really no liars or lies after all,
And that nothing fails its perfect return, and that what are called
    lies are perfect returns,
And that each thing exactly represents itself and what has
    preceded it,
And that the truth includes all, and is compact just as much as
    space is compact,
And that there is no flaw or vacuum in the amount of the truth
    — but that all is truth without exception;
And henceforth I will go celebrate any thing I see or am,
And sing and laugh and deny nothing.

THE BOOK OF HEAVENLY DEATH

CIV

They shall arise in the States,
They shall report Nature, laws, physiology, and happiness,
They shall illustrate Democracy and the kosmos,
They shall be alimentive, amative, perceptive,
They shall be complete women and men, their pose brawny and
    supple, their drink water, their blood clean and clear,
They shall fully enjoy materialism and the sight of products,
    they shall enjoy the sight of the beef, lumber, bread-stuffs,
    of Chicago the great city,
They shall train themselves to go in public to become orators
    and oratresses,
Strong and sweet shall their tongues be, poems and materials
    of poems shall come from their lives, they shall be makers
    and finders,
Of them and of their works shall emerge divine conveyers, to
    convey gospels,
Characters, events, retrospections, shall be convey'd in gospels,
    trees, animals, waters, shall be convey'd,
Death, the future, the invisible faith, shall all be convey'd.

CV

Weave in, weave in, my hardy life,
Weave yet a soldier strong and full for great campaigns to come,
Weave in red blood, weave sinews in like ropes, the senses,
    sight weave in,

THE BOOK OF HEAVENLY DEATH

Weave lasting sure, weave day and night the weft, the warp,
    incessant weave, tire not,
(We know not what the use O life, nor know the aim, the end,
    nor really aught we know,
But know the work, the need goes on and shall go on, the
    death-envelop'd march of peace as well as war goes on,)
For great campaigns of peace the same the wiry threads to
    weave,
We know not why or what, yet weave, forever weave.

CVI

But I too announce solid things,
Science, ships, politics, cities, factories, are not nothing,
Like a grand procession to music of distant bugles pouring,
    triumphantly moving, and grander heaving in sight,
They stand for realities — all is as it should be.

Then my realities;
What else is so real as mine?
Libertad and the divine average, freedom to every slave on the
    face of the earth,
The rapt promises and luminè of seers, the spiritual world, these
    centuries-lasting songs,
And our visions, the visions of poets, the most solid announce-
    ments of any.

THE BOOK OF HEAVENLY DEATH

CVII

This is thy hour O Soul, thy free flight into the wordless,
Away from books, away from art, the day erased, the lesson done,
Thee fully forth emerging, silent, gazing, pondering the themes
    thou lovest best,
Night, sleep, death and the stars.

CVIII

Sweet are the blooming cheeks of the living — sweet are the
    musical voices sounding,
But sweet, ah sweet, are the dead with their silent eyes.

Dearest comrades, all is over and long gone,
But love is not over — and what love, O comrades!
Perfume from battle-fields rising, up from the fœtor arising.

Perfume therefore my chant, O love, immortal love,
Give me to bathe the memories of all dead soldiers,
Shroud them, embalm them, cover them all over with tender pride.

Perfume all — make all wholesome,
Make these ashes to nourish and blossom,
O love, solve all, fructify all with the last chemistry.

Give me exhaustless, make me a fountain,
That I exhale love from me wherever I go like a moist perennial
    dew.

84

THE BOOK OF HEAVENLY DEATH

CIX

Splendor of ended day floating and filling me,
Hour prophetic, hour resuming the past,
Inflating my throat, you divine average,
You earth and life till the last ray gleams I sing.

Open mouth of my soul uttering gladness,
Eyes of my soul seeing perfection,
Natural life of me faithfully praising things,
Corroborating forever the triumph of things.

Illustrious every one !
Illustrious what we name space, sphere of unnumber'd spirits,
Illustrious the mystery of motion in all beings, even the tiniest
     insect,
Illustrious the attribute of speech, the senses, the body,
Illustrious the passing light—illustrious the pale reflection on
     the new moon in the western sky,
Illustrious whatever I see or hear or touch, to the last.

Good in all,
In the satisfaction and aplomb of animals,
In the annual return of the seasons,
In the hilarity of youth,
In the strength and flush of manhood,
In the grandeur and exquisiteness of old age,
In the superb vistas of death.

THE BOOK OF HEAVENLY DEATH

Wonderful to depart!
Wonderful to be here!
The heart, to jet the all-alike and innocent blood!
To breathe the air, how delicious!
To speak — to walk — to seize something by the hand!
To prepare for sleep, for bed, to look on my rose-color'd flesh!
To be conscious of my body, so satisfied, so large!
To be this incredible God I am!
To have gone forth among other Gods, these men and women
    I love.

Wonderful how I celebrate you and myself!
How my thoughts play subtly at the spectacles around!
How the clouds pass silently overhead!
How the earth darts on and on! and how the sun, moon, stars,
    dart on and on!
How the water sports and sings! (surely it is alive!)
How the trees rise and stand up, with strong trunks, with
    branches and leaves!
(Surely there is something more in each of the trees, some living
    soul.)

O amazement of things — even the least particle!
O spirituality of things!

CX

I sing to the last the equalities modern or old,
I sing the endless finalés of things,

THE BOOK OF HEAVENLY DEATH

I say Nature continues, glory continues,
I praise with electric voice,
For I do not see one imperfection in the universe,
And I do not see one cause or result lamentable at last in the
    universe.

CXI

To Nature encompassing these, encompassing God — to the
    joyous, electric all,
To the sense of Death, and accepting exulting in Death in its
    turn the same as life,
The entrance of man to sing;
To compact you, ye parted, diverse lives,
To put rapport the mountains and rocks and streams,
And the winds of the north, and the forests of oak and pine,
With you O soul.

CXII

The untold want by life and land ne'er granted,
Now voyager sail thou forth to seek and find.

CXIII

What are those of the known but to ascend and enter the
    Unknown ?
And what are those of life but for Death ?

THE BOOK OF HEAVENLY DEATH

CXIV

These carols sung to cheer my passage through the world I see,
For completion I dedicate to the Invisible World.

CXV

I have press'd through in my own right,
I have sung the body and the soul, war and peace have I sung,
    and the songs of life and death,
And the songs of birth, and shown that there are many births.

CXVI

I announce a life that shall be copious, vehement, spiritual, bold,
I announce an end that shall lightly and joyfully meet its trans-
    lation.

CXVII

So I pass, a little time vocal, visible, contrary,
Afterward a melodious echo, passionately bent for, (death making
    me really undying,)
The best of me then when no longer visible, for toward that I
    have been incessantly preparing.

What is there more, that I lag and pause and crouch extended
    with unshut mouth?
Is there a single final farewell?

THE BOOK OF HEAVENLY DEATH

My songs cease, I abandon them,
From behind the screen where I hid I advance personally solely
    to you.

Camerado, this is no book,
Who touches this touches a man,
(Is it night? are we here together alone?)
It is I you hold and who holds you,
I spring from the pages into your arms — decease calls me forth.

CXVIII

Dear friend whoever you are take this kiss,
I give it especially to you, do not forget me,
I feel like one who has done work for the day to retire awhile,
I receive now again of my many translations, from my avataras
    ascending, while others doubtless await me,
An unknown sphere more real than I dream'd, more direct,
    darts awakening rays about me, *So long!*
Remember my words, I may again return,
I love you, I depart from materials,
I am as one disembodied, triumphant, dead.

CXIX

Last of ebb, and daylight waning,
Scented sea-cool landward making, smells of sedge and salt
    incoming,

THE BOOK OF HEAVENLY DEATH

With many a half-caught voice sent up from the eddies,
Many a muffled confession — many a sob and whisper'd word,
As of speakers far or hid.

How they sweep down and out ! how they mutter !
Poets unnamed — artists greatest of any, with cherish'd lost
    designs,
Love's unresponse — a chorus of age's complaints — hope's last
    words,
Some suicide's despairing cry, *Away to the boundless waste, and
never again return.*

On to oblivion then !
On, on, and do your part, ye burying, ebbing tide !
On for your time, ye furious debouché !

And yet not you alone, twilight and burying ebb,
Nor you, ye lost designs alone — nor failures, aspirations ;
I know, divine deceitful ones, your glamour's seeming ;
Duly by you, from you, the tide and light again — duly the hinges
    turning,
Duly the needed discord-parts offsetting, blending,
Weaving from you, from Sleep, Night, Death itself,
The rhythmus of Birth eternal.

CXX

Nothing is ever really lost, or can be lost,
No birth, identity, form — no object of the world.

Nor life, nor force, nor any visible thing;
Appearance must not foil, nor shifted sphere confuse thy brain.
Ample are time and space — ample the fields of Nature.
The body, sluggish, aged, cold — the embers left from earlier
    fires,
The light in the eye grown dim, shall duly flame again;
The sun now low in the west rises for mornings and for noons
    continual;
To frozen clods ever the spring's invisible law returns,
With grass and flowers and summer fruits and corn.

CXXI

My science-friend, my noblest woman-friend,
(Now buried in an English grave — and this a memory-leaf for
    her dear sake,)
Ended our talk — " The sum, concluding all we know of old or
    modern learning, intuitions deep,
" Of all Geologies — Histories — of all Astronomy — of Evolu-
    tion, Metaphysics all,
Is, that we all are onward, onward, speeding slowly, surely
    bettering,
Life, life an endless march, an endless army, (no halt, but it is
    duly over,)
The world, the race, the soul — in space and time the universes,
All bound as is befitting each — all surely going somewhere."

THE BOOK OF HEAVENLY DEATH

CXXII

Grand is the seen, the light, to me—grand are the sky and stars,
Grand is the earth, and grand are lasting time and space,
And grand their laws, so multiform, puzzling, evolutionary;
But grander far the unseen soul of me, comprehending, endow-
　　ing all those,
Lighting the light, the sky and stars, delving the earth, sailing
　　the sea,
(What were all those, indeed, without thee, unseen soul? of
　　what amount without thee?)
More evolutionary, vast, puzzling, O my soul!
More multiform far—more lasting thou than they.

CXXIII

Good-bye my Fancy!
Farewell dear mate, dear love!
I'm going away, I know not where,
Or to what fortune, or whether I may ever see you again,
So Good-bye my Fancy.

Now for my last—let me look back a moment;
The slower fainter ticking of the clock is in me,
Exit, nightfall, and soon the heart-thud stopping.

Long have we lived, joy'd, caress'd together;
Delightful!—now separation—Good-bye my Fancy.

THE BOOK OF HEAVENLY DEATH

Yet let me not be too hasty,
Long indeed have we lived, slept, filter'd, become really blended
    into one;
Then if we die we die together, (yes, we'll remain one,)
If we go anywhere we'll go together to meet what happens,
May-be we'll be better off and blither, and learn something,
May-be it is yourself now really ushering me to the true songs,
    (who knows?)
May-be it is you the mortal knob really undoing, turning—so
    now finally,
Good-bye—and hail! my Fancy.

CXXIV

One thought ever at the fore —
That in the Divine Ship, the World, breasting Time and Space,
All Peoples of the globe together sail, sail the same voyage, are
    bound to the same destination.

CXXV

While behind all, firm and erect as ever,
Undismay'd amid the rapids —amid the irresistible and deadly
    urge,
Stands a helmsman, with brow elate and strong hand.

CXXVI

Nay, do not dream, designer dark,
Thou hast portray'd or hit thy theme entire;

THE BOOK OF HEAVENLY DEATH

I, hoverer of late by this dark valley, by its confines, having
    glimpses of it,
Here enter lists with thee, claiming my right to make a symbol
    too.
For I have seen many wounded soldiers die,
After dread suffering — have seen their lives pass off with smiles;
And I have watch'd the death-hours of the old; and seen the
    infant die;
The rich, with all his nurses and his doctors;
And then the poor, in meagreness and poverty;
And I myself for long, O Death, have breath'd my every breath
Amid the nearness and the silent thought of thee.

And out of these and thee,
I make a scene, a song (not fear of thee,
Nor gloom's ravines, nor bleak, nor dark — for I do not fear
    thee,
Nor celebrate the struggle, or contortion, or hard-tied knot),
Of the broad blessed light and perfect air, with meadows, rip-
    pling tides, and trees and flowers and grass,
And the low hum of living breeze — and in the midst God's
    beautiful eternal right hand,
Thee, holiest minister of Heaven — thee, envoy, usherer, guide
    at last of all,
Rich, florid, loosener of the stricture-knot call'd life,
Sweet, peaceful, welcome Death.

THE BOOK OF HEAVENLY DEATH

CXXVII

Now finalè to the shore,
Now land and life finalè and farewell,
Now Voyager depart, (much, much for thee is yet in store,)
Often enough hast thou adventur'd o'er the seas,
Cautiously cruising, studying the charts,
Duly again to port and hawser's tie returning;
But now obey thy cherish'd secret wish,
Embrace thy friends, leave all in order,
To port and hawser's tie no more returning,
Depart upon thy endless cruise old Sailor.

CXXVIII

Joy, shipmate, joy!
(Pleas'd to my soul at death I cry,)
Our life is closed, our life begins,
The long, long anchorage we leave,
The ship is clear at last, she leaps!
She swiftly courses from the shore,
Joy, shipmate, joy.

It has been thought desirable by the publisher to print the following Index, reference being made to the sections instead of pages throughout this book. Taken in connection with the Table of Contents each citation can thus be readily verified from the authorized edition of *Leaves of Grass*, issued by Small, Maynard and Company, Boston.

T. B. M.

INDEX

INDEX

INDEX

INDEX

INDEX

CPSIA information can be obtained
at www.ICGtesting.com
Printed in the USA
BVHW050202110719
553087BV00005B/65/P

9 780469 921429